Seitan Cookbook Recipes

Flavorful No-Meat Seitan Recipes that Are High in Protein and Low in Calories

Jenny Kern

Table Of Contents

Introduction

Thank you very much for purchasing this cookbook. The name Seitan evokes flavors and distant countries, so much so that its origin is lost among the Chinese Buddhist monks, centuries ago, and has always represented one of the cornerstones of oriental cuisine.

Obtained from wheat flour, rinsed and kneaded until only gluten remains, then boiled in flavored water and flavored in different ways, seitan is a pleasant food with a delicate flavor, known to all of us vegetarians because it lends itself to countless uses and its versatility makes it the main ingredient of a healthy and cruelty-free cuisine. Often people react suspiciously of its exotic name, expecting who knows what strange concoction - it's just an equivocal sound! I hope that the recipes I am about to propose to you will be to your liking.

Enjoy your meal!

Breakfast Recipes

1. Healthy Celery Loaf

Preparation Time: 2 hours 40 minutes

Cooking time: 50 minutes

Servings: 1 loaf

Ingredients:

1 can (10 ounces) cream of celery soup

3 tbsp low-fat milk, heated

1 tbsp vegetable oil

1¼ tsp celery salt

¾ cup celery, fresh/sliced thin

1 tbsp celery leaves, fresh, chopped

1 whole egg

¼ tsp sugar

3 cups bread flour

¼ tsp ginger

½ cup quick-cooking oats

2 tbsp gluten

2 tsp celery seeds

1 pack of active dry yeast

Directions:

1. Add all the ingredients to your bread machine, carefully following the instructions of the manufacturer.
2. Set the program of your bread machine to Basic/White Bread and set crust type to Medium.
3. Press START and wait until the cycle completes.
4. Once the loaf is ready, take the bucket out and let the loaf cool for 5 minutes.
5. Gently shake the bucket to remove the loaf.
6. Transfer to a cooling rack, slice, and serve. Enjoy!

2. Seitan Cakes with Broccoli Mash

Preparation Time: 10 Minutes

Cooking Time: 20 Minutes

Servings: 4

Ingredients:

1 tbsp flax seed powder

1 ½ lb. crumbled seitan

½ white onion

2 oz olive oil

1 lb. broccoli

5 oz cold plant butter

2 oz grated plant-based Parmesan

4 oz plant butter, room temperature

2 tbsp lemon juice

Directions:

1. Preheat oven to 220 F. In a bowl, mix the flax seed powder with 3 tbsp water and allow sitting to thicken for 5 minutes.
2. When the vegan "flax egg" is ready, add in crumbled seitan, white onion, salt, and pepper.
3. Mix and mold out 6-8 cakes out of the mixture.

4. Melt plant butter in a skillet and fry the patties on both sides until golden brown. Remove onto a wire rack to cool slightly.
5. Pour salted water into a pot, bring to a boil, and add in broccoli. Cook until the broccoli is tender but not too soft. Drain and transfer to a bowl.
6. Add in cold plant butter, plant-based Parmesan, salt, and pepper.
7. Puree the ingredients until smooth and creamy. Set aside.
8. Mix the soft plant butter with lemon juice, salt, and pepper in a bowl.
9. Serve the seitan cakes with the broccoli mash and lemon butter.

3. Basil Pesto Seitan Panini

Preparation Time: 10 Minutes

Cooking Time: 20 Minutes

Servings: 4

Ingredients:

For the Seitan:

⅔ cup basil pesto

½ lemon, juiced

1 garlic clove, minced

⅛ tsp salt

1 cup chopped seitan

For the Panini:

3 tbsp basil pesto

8 thick slices of whole-wheat ciabatta

Olive oil for brushing

8 slices plant-based mozzarella

1 yellow bell pepper, chopped

¼ cup grated plant Parmesan cheese

Directions:

1. In a medium bowl, mix the pesto, lemon juice, garlic, and salt. Add the seitan and coat well with the marinade. Cover with plastic wrap and marinate in the refrigerator for 30 minutes.

2. Preheat a large skillet over medium heat and remove the seitan from the fridge. Cook the seitan in the skillet until brown and cooked through, 2-3 minutes. Turn the heat off.

3. Preheat a panini press to medium heat.

4. In a small bowl, mix the pesto in the inner parts of two slices of bread. On the outer parts, apply some olive oil and place a slice with (the olive oil side down) in the press.

5. Lay 2 slices of plant-based mozzarella cheese on the bread, spoon some seitan on top. Sprinkle with some bell pepper and some plant-based Parmesan cheese. Cover with another bread slice.

6. Close the press and grill the bread for 1 to 2 minutes. Flip the bread, and grill further for 1 minute or until the cheese melts and golden brown on both sides. Serve warm.

4. Seitan Cauliflower Gratin

Preparation Time: 10 Minutes

Cooking Time: 20 Minutes

Servings: 4

Ingredients:

2 oz plant butter

1 leek, coarsely chopped

1 white onion, coarsely chopped

2 cups broccoli florets

1 cup cauliflower florets

2 cups crumbled seitan

1 cup coconut cream

2 tbsp mustard powder

5 oz grated plant-based Parmesan

4 tbsp fresh rosemary

1 tsp Salt and black pepper to taste

Directions:

1. Preheat oven to 450°F.
2. Melt half of the plant butter in a pot over medium heat. Add in leek, white onion, broccoli, and cauliflower, and cook for about 6 minutes. Transfer the vegetables to a baking dish.
3. Melt the remaining butter in a skillet over medium heat and cook the seitan until browned.
4. Mix the coconut cream and mustard powder in a bowl. Pour the mixture over the vegetables.
5. Scatter the seitan and plant-based Parmesan cheese on top and sprinkle with rosemary, salt, and pepper.
6. Bake for 15 minutes. Remove to cool for a few minutes and serve.

5. Hot Seitan with Rice

Preparation Time: 10 Minutes

Cooking Time: 20 Minutes

Servings: 4

Ingredients:

2 tbsp olive oil

1 lb. seitan, cut into cubes

Salt and black pepper to taste

1 tsp chili powder

1 tsp onion powder

1 tsp cumin powder

1 tsp garlic powder

1 yellow onion, chopped

2 celery stalks, chopped

2 carrots diced

4-5 cloves garlic

1 cup vegetable broth

1 tsp oregano

1 cup chopped tomatoes

3 green chilies, chopped

1 lime, juiced

1 cup brown rice

Directions:

1. Add brown rice, 2 cups of water, and salt to a pot. Cook for 15-20 minutes.
2. Heat the olive oil in a large pot, season the seitan with salt, black pepper, and cook in the oil until brown, 10 minutes.
3. Stir in the chili powder, onion powder, cumin powder, garlic powder, and cook until fragrant, 1 minute.
4. Mix in the onion, celery, carrots, garlic, and cook until softened. Pour in the vegetable broth, 1 cup of water, oregano, tomatoes, and green chilies.
5. Cover the pot and cook until the tomatoes soften, and the liquid reduces by half, 10 to 15 minutes.
6. Open the lid, adjust the taste with salt, black pepper, and mix in the lime juice. Dish and serve warm with brown rice.

6. Saucy Seitan with Sesame Seeds

Preparation Time: 10 Minutes

Cooking Time: 20 Minutes

Servings: 4

Ingredients:

4 tsp olive oil

½ tsp freshly grated ginger

3 garlic cloves, minced

⅓ tsp red chili flakes

⅓ tsp allspice

½ cup soy sauce

½ cup + 2 tbsp pure date sugar

2 tsp cornstarch

1 ½ tbsp olive oil

1 lb. seitan, cut into 1-inch pieces

1 tbsp toasted sesame seeds

1 tbsp sliced scallions

Directions:

1. Heat half of the olive oil in a wok and sauté ginger and garlic until fragrant, 30 seconds.

2. Mix in red chili flakes, allspice, soy sauce, and date sugar. Allow the sugar to melt and set aside.

3. In a small bowl, mix cornstarch and 2 tbsp of water. Stir the cornstarch mixture into the sauce and allow thickening for 1 minute.

4. Heat the remaining olive oil in a medium skillet over medium heat and fry the seitan on both sides until crispy, 10 minutes.

5. Mix the seitan into the sauce and warm over low heat. Dish the food, garnish with sesame seeds and scallions. Serve warm.

7. Seitan & Lentil Chili

Preparation Time: 10 Minutes

Cooking Time: 20 Minutes

Servings: 4

Ingredients:

2 tbsp olive oil

1 onion, chopped

8 oz seitan, chopped

1 cup lentils

1 (14.5-oz) can diced tomatoes

1 tbsp soy sauce

1 tbsp chili powder

1 tsp ground cumin

1 tsp ground allspice

½ tsp ground oregano

¼ tsp ground cayenne

1 tsp Salt and black pepper to taste

Directions:

1. Heat the oil in a pot over medium heat. Place in onion and seitan and cook for 10 minutes.
2. Add in lentils, diced tomatoes, 2 cups of water, soy sauce, chili powder, cumin, allspice, sugar, oregano, cayenne pepper, salt, and pepper.
3. Bring to a boil, then lower the heat and simmer for 20 minutes.

Nibbles and Bites Recipes

8. Italian Seitan Marinara Burgers

Preparation Time: 10 Minutes

Cooking Time: 30 Minutes

Servings: 4

Ingredients:

1 cup vegetable broth

2 tbsp olive oil

1 ¼ cups vital wheat gluten

½ cup all-purpose flour

¼ cup nutritional yeast

1 tbsp Italian seasoning

¾ cup marinara sauce

6 slices vegan mozzarella cheese

Directions:

1. Preheat oven to 375F. In a small bowl, whisk together vegetable broth and olive oil.

2. In a large bowl, combine vital wheat gluten, flour, nutritional yeast, and Italian seasoning. Pour in broth mixture and knead the dough until smooth.

3. Divide dough into 6 equal-sized pieces, and form each into patties. Place seitan on a baking sheet and bake for 30-35 minutes.

4. Top burger with 1 slice vegan cheese and 2 tbsp of marinara sauce.

9. Italian Bruschetta Burgers

Preparation Time: 10 Minutes

Cooking Time: 30 Minutes

Servings: 4

Ingredients:

1 cup vegetable broth

2 tbsp olive oil

1 ¼ cups vital wheat gluten

½ cup all-purpose flour

¼ cup nutritional yeast

1 tbsp Italian seasoning

6 slices vegan mozzarella cheese

1 large tomato, diced

2 tbsp fresh basil, chopped

1 tbsp balsamic vinegar

Directions:

1. Preheat oven to 375F. In a small bowl, whisk together broth and olive oil.

2. In a large bowl, combine vital wheat gluten, flour, nutritional yeast, and seasoning.
3. Pour in broth mixture and knead the dough until smooth. Divide dough into 6 equal-sized pieces and flatten each into a patty. Place burgers onto a large baking sheet.
4. Bake for 30-35 minutes. Mix diced tomato, basil, and balsamic vinegar together.
5. Place burger patties on the bottom of a hamburger bun, top with one slice vegan cheese, and 1 tbsp of bruschetta mixture.

10.   Barbecue Seitan Burgers

Preparation Time: 10 Minutes

Cooking Time: 30 Minutes

Servings: 4

Ingredients:

1 cup textured vegetable protein

1 tbsp vegan Worcestershire sauce

1 ¼ cups vital wheat gluten

½ cup chickpea flour

¼ cup nutritional yeast

1 tbsp Montreal chicken seasoning

¼ cup barbecue sauce

Directions:

1. Preheat oven to 375F. In a small bowl, whisk together vegetable broth and vegan Worcestershire sauce.
2. In a large bowl, combine vital wheat gluten, chickpea flour, nutritional yeast, and chicken seasoning.
3. Add in broth mixture and barbecue sauce. Knead dough until smooth.
4. Divide dough into 6 equal-sized pieces, form each into patties, place onto a large baking sheet. Bake for 30-35 minutes.

11.Seitan "Chicken Burgers

Preparation Time: 10 Minutes

Cooking Time: 30 Minutes

Servings: 4

Ingredients:

¾ cup vegetable broth

¼ cup pickle juice

1 tbsp vegan Worcestershire sauce

1 ¼ cups vital wheat gluten

½ cup chickpea flour

¼ cup nutritional yeast

1 tbsp Montreal chicken seasoning

1 cup panko breadcrumbs

¼ cup nutritional yeast

Directions:

1. Preheat oven to 375F. In a small bowl, whisk together vegetable broth, pickle juice, and vegan Worcestershire sauce.

2. In a large bowl, mix vital wheat gluten, chickpea flour, nutritional yeast, and seasoning.

3. Pour in broth mixture and mix until a dough forms. Knead dough until smooth. Divide dough into 6 equal-sized pieces and form each into patties.

4. In a shallow dish, whisk together breadcrumbs and nutritional yeast. Coat each seitan patty in mixture and place on a greased baking sheet. Bake for 30-35 minutes, flipping halfway through.

12.   Queso Seitan Burgers

Preparation Time: 10 Minutes

Cooking Time: 30 Minutes

Servings: 4

Ingredients:

1 cup vegetable broth

2 tbsp olive oil

1 ¼ cups vital wheat gluten

½ cup chickpea flour

¼ cup nutritional yeast

2 tsp taco seasoning

3 tbsp vegan butter

2 tbsp all-purpose flour

1 cup unsweetened almond milk

½ cup nutritional yeast

½ tsp salt

¼ tsp ground black pepper

⅔ cup salsa

Directions:

1. Preheat oven to 375F. In a small bowl, whisk together vegetable broth and olive oil. In a large bowl, combine vital wheat gluten, chickpea flour, nutritional yeast, and taco seasoning.

2. Pour in broth mixture and mix until a dough forms. Knead dough until smooth. Divide dough into 6 equal-sized pieces and form each into patties. Place burgers onto a greased baking sheet. Bake for 30-35 minutes, flipping halfway through.

3. In a large saucepan, melt vegan butter over medium heat, add in flour and cook for a minute to brown. Add in almond milk, nutritional yeast, salt, and pepper. Cook over medium heat until thickened.

4. Remove from heat and stir in salsa. Top burgers with queso.

13.   Cassoeula

Preparation Time: 10 Minutes

Cooking Time: 30 Minutes

Servings: 4

Ingredients:

400 gr of seitan,

500 gr of Savoy cabbage, one onion, 3 carrots, 3 ribs of celery,

3 tbsp of extra virgin olive oil, vegetable stock (see recipe), salt, pepper

Directions:

1. Peel the cabbage and remove the core. Cook it for about half an hour. Finely chop the onion and brown it in a pan with oil. Add the sliced carrots and celery.
2. Add the seitan cut into pieces and floured, then brown. While cooking, pour in white wine, add the tomato, then the stock, and cook for 10 minutes.

14.   Tilapia Tacos

Preparation Time: 10 Minutes

Cooking Time: 30 Minutes

Servings: 4

Ingredients:

3 (4-ounce) tilapia fillets, clean

Sea salt, to taste

Black pepper, to taste

2 tbsp butter

1 cup shredded cabbage

½ cup chopped cilantro

⅓ cup chopped mint

2 tbsp fresh lime juice

4 flour tortillas, warm

1 cup fresh salsa (optional)

Directions:

1. Season the tilapia with salt and pepper. Heat a large skillet over medium heat and melt butter in it.
2. Cook the fillets for 2 minutes per side. Remove from the pan and set aside. Chop the fish before serving into bite-sized pieces.
3. Toss the remaining ingredients together in a bowl. Warm the tortillas and then top with tilapia and cabbage mixture.

Lunch Recipes

15.   Easy Seitan for Two

Preparation Time: 10 Minutes

Cooking Time: 30 Minutes

Servings: 4

Ingredients

½ tsp freshly ground black pepper

Pinch of fine sea salt

2 (every 4 ounces, or 113 g) Kind-to- Cows Seitan cutlets

⅓ cup (80 ml) vegetable broth

1 tbsp (16 g) tomato paste

1 tsp balsamic vinegar

1 tsp Dijon mustard

1 tsp white miso

1 tbsp (15 ml) high heat neutral-flavored oil

2 tbsp (20 g) minced shallot

Directions:

1. Rub the pepper and salt evenly into the seitan cutlets. Whisk together the broth, tomato paste, vinegar, mustard, and miso in a small bowl.
2. Heat the oil over medium-high heat in a large skillet. Put the cutlets into the skillet and cook for 3 to 5 minutes, until browned.
3. Turnover and cook the second side for 3 to 4 minutes until also browned. Remove the cutlets and set them aside. Reduce the heat to medium-low. Add the shallots. Cook and stir for 2 to 3 minutes, until softened.
4. Be careful not to burn them. Scrape up any bits stuck to the skillet. Pour the broth mixture into the skillet. Bring to a simmer and stir for 3 to 4 minutes.
5. Put the cutlets back into the skillet and turn to coat. Simmer for 3 to 4 minutes to heat the cutlets throughout. Spoon the sauce over the cutlets to serve.

16.   Seitan with Peas

Preparation Time: 15 minutes

Cooking Time: 50 minutes

Servings: 4

Ingredients:

500 g seitan,

A tin of medium peas, a clove of garlic,

One onion,

Vegetable stock cube,

Shoyu, kuzu, parsley

Directions:

1. Cook the peas in a saucepan with plenty of onion, a clove of garlic, and a vegetable stock cube.
2. When the peas are almost cooked, add the seitan cut into strips and, if necessary, a tbsp of kuzu, so that it tastes better.
3. Cook for ten minutes, then add a tbsp of shoyu and serve garnished with parsley.

17.   Seitan with Cream of Mushroom Soup

Preparation Time: 15 minutes

Cooking Time: 50 minutes

Servings: 4

Ingredients:

400 g seitan,

2 garlic cloves,

4 or 5 mint leaves,

350 g Mushrooms,

5 tbsp extra virgin olive oil, 1 tbsp shoyu,

Salt, 3 tbsp soy yogurt

Directions:

1. Crush the garlic and place it in a pan with the oil, warming it slightly without browning, then add the sliced mushrooms and cook for about 15 minutes.
2. Cut the seitan into small pieces and place in the pan with the mint.
3. Cook for another 10 minutes and season with salt, shoyu, and soy yogurt which, as it congeals, will form a delicate cream.

18. Seitan with Dried Mushroom Sauce

Preparation Time: 15 minutes

Cooking Time: 50 minutes

Servings: 4

Ingredients:

500 g of grilled seitan,

A bag of dried porcini mushrooms,

2 shallots, 2 carrots,

A stalk of celery, shoyu

2 tbsp Kuzu, extra virgin olive oil

Directions:

1. Soak the mushrooms in a cup of warm water to revive them.
2. Finely slice the shallots, carrots, and celery and sauté in a pan with 3 tbsp of extra virgin olive oil.
3. Cut the seitan into slices, not too thin, and add it to the sauté. Cook for five minutes to allow the seitan to take on flavor, stirring occasionally.
4. Squeeze out the soaked mushrooms and add them to the seitan. Season to taste with shoyu and let stew until mushrooms are soft; add their soaking water if necessary to keep them from sticking. In the meantime, in a glass of cold water, mix well a level tbsp of kuzu.
5. Add it to the seitan with the mushrooms to form a fairly thick sauce. Serve with polenta.

19. Mediterranean Seitan

Preparation Time: 15 minutes

Cooking Time: 50 minutes

Servings: 4

Ingredients:

400 gr of seitan,

300 gr of peeled tomatoes, one leek,

2 tbsp of olive paste,

2 tsp fresh grated ginger,

3 tbsp coarsely chopped almonds, dried basil, extra virgin olive oil

Directions:

1. Cut the seitan into strips. Sauté the thinly sliced leek in a pan with three tbsp of oil over low heat for 2-3 minutes. At this point, add the ginger, diced tomato, and basil, stir, and sauté for a minute.
2. Then add the olive paste, chopped almonds, seitan with a little of its soaking water, cover, and cook for another 2-3 minutes.
3. Before serving, leave the pan covered for another 2 minutes.

Soup and Stews Recipes

20.   Shelf Paper Soup

Preparation Time: 15 minutes

Cooking Time: 50 minutes

Servings: 4

Ingredients:

1 can kidney beans

1 can diced tomatoes

4-5 cups water (and or seitan broth)

1 strip kombu (opt)

½ cup chopped onion

3-4 cloves diced garlic

3 Tbsp uncooked barley

¼ cup spaghetti or other pasta, broken into bite-sized bits

½ diced or ground seitan or seitan salami

Leftover veggies – clean out the frig

1 Tbsp olive oil

2 tbsp Salt, pepper, and other seasonings to taste

Directions:

1. Put all the ingredients in a pot, bring to a boil, reduce and simmer for about an hour.

21.   Pot Roast Soup

Preparation Time: 15 minutes

Cooking Time: 50 minutes

Servings: 4

Ingredients:

1-2 cups seitan, cut into bite-sized pieces (brown in a little oil first for extra color and firmness if desired)

4-5 small red, white or yellow potatoes cut into chunks (no need to peel)

2-3 medium carrots, cut into bite-sized pieces

1 cup onion, chopped

1-2 Tbsp olive oil

¼ cup soy sauce or Bragg Liquid Aminos

¼ cup red wine

4-6 cups water (or seitan or veggie broth)

2 tbsp Oregano, pepper, basil, etc. To taste

Directions:

1. Put all ingredients in a large pot. Add water or broth if needed to cover all ingredients.
2. Bring to a boil, reduce to a simmer and cook for about 30 minutes or until veggies are tender.
3. Served with some bread and a salad, this is a meal in itself.

22.   Seitan Stew with Peas And Polenta

Preparation Time: 15 minutes

Cooking Time: 50 minutes

Servings: 4

Ingredients:

400 gr of seitan,

250 gr instant polenta,

250 g peas,

1 garlic clove,

Vegetable stock (see recipe),

4 tbsp extra virgin olive oil,

Spelt flour,

Tamari,

Salt and pepper

Directions:

1. Drain the seitan and cut it into pieces, then dip in flour. Sauté the garlic for a few minutes and add the seitan; brown it and then add a little stock.

2. Allow the stock to dry up and add the peas and a few drops of tamari to add flavor. Cook for 5 minutes, then turn off the heat and allow to rest. In the meantime, bring one liter of water with a little salt to a boil.
3. When it boils, slowly pour in the polenta while stirring, continue stirring for two minutes, then turn off the heat.
4. Serve the polenta hot adding the seitan with peas warm. Season with salt and pepper to taste.

Dinner Recipes

23. Zighinì

Preparation Time: 15 minutes

Cooking Time: 20 minutes

Servings: 4

Ingredients:

500 g seitan cut into chunks,

One onion,

2 cloves of garlic,

A tbsp of extra virgin olive oil,

3 tbsp of berberé (see recipe) or one hot pepper,

One glass of water,

Salt,

500 g of peeled tomatoes

Directions:

1. Wilt a large onion and two chopped garlic cloves in a non-stick pan. Cover the pan and after five minutes add a tbsp

of extra virgin olive oil, three tbsp of berberè, a glass of water, and salt.

2. Allow to reduce slowly, then add the peeled tomatoes and, if necessary, another glass of water.

3. Continue to simmer for 15 minutes. Add the chopped seitan and finish cooking until the bottom has reduced.

Traditional spicy recipe from Eritrean cuisine. A unique dish that is traditionally eaten on injera, the typical Ethiopian bread, so that it soaks up the sauce.

24.   Exotic Marinated Seitan Steak

Preparation Time: 15 minutes

Cooking Time: 20 minutes

Servings: 4

Ingredients:

500 g seitan

1 large onion

70 g fresh ginger

4 chili peppers

10 cloves garlic

4 tbsp olive oil

3 colorful peppers

1 tbsp thyme

½ tsp nutmeg

1 tsp cinnamon

1 tsp allspice

½ tsp clove

4 tbsp lime juice

Directions:

1. Cut the onion and garlic into small cubes. Finely grate the ginger. Mix the spices, divide, and mix one half with the onion, garlic, ginger, and lime juice to make a marinade.
2. Cut the seitan into equal-sized steaks, coat with the marinade, and refrigerate for at least 2 hours, preferably 8 hours.
3. Sear the marinated steaks in olive oil in a pan until hot. Then place the steaks on a baking sheet.
4. Add the peppers cut into strips and whole chili peppers. Season with the second half and cook in the oven at 180° C for about 10 - 15 minutes. Rice or pita bread is suitable as a side dish.

25.   Seitan and Onion Gyros

Preparation Time: 15 minutes

Cooking Time: 20 minutes

Servings: 4

Ingredients:

200 g seitan

1 tbsp gyros spice

30 g canola oil

1 large onion fresh

20 g canola oil

For the Rice Garnish:

1 cup of rice

2 cups of water

1 bowl of grated carrots

2 tsp vegetable broth

Directions:

1. Cut the seitan into strips and soak in the gyros spice for about 4-8 hours.
2. For the rice side dish, boil the rice in the water with the vegetable broth. Simmer for about 10 minutes and then add the shredded carrots.
3. Halve the large onion and cut it into rings. Sauté in hot oil. At the same time, fry the seitan strips in the oil until crispy. Mix both and serve with rice garnish. Serve with a salad.

26. African Goulash with Chickpeas And Seitan

Preparation Time: 15 minutes

Cooking Time: 20 minutes

Servings: 4

Ingredients

500 g seitan

6 tomatoes

1 can chickpeas

4 onions

4 cloves of garlic

1 tbsp of tomato paste

3 tsp cumin

1 tsp cayenne pepper

1 fresh chili pepper

1 tbsp olive oil

Salt and pepper

1 tbsp Ras el-Hanout

1 bunch flat-leaf parsley

200 g peeled cashew nuts

Vegetable broth as needed.

Directions:

1. Peel and dice the onions. Dice the seitan and fry it with olive oil in a high pot. When well browned, add onions and sauté. Peel garlic and add with a garlic press. Wash and dice tomatoes.
2. When onions are sufficiently browned, deglaze with diced tomatoes and add vegetable broth if necessary. Let

simmer on low heat for at least 3 hours, stirring, adding vegetable broth if needed.

3. Meanwhile, in a blender, puree cashews until creamy, add tomato paste and remaining spices, and stir vigorously. Add this seasoning paste to the goulash and about 40 minutes before the end of the cooking time, add the chickpeas to the goulash.

4. Before serving, season to taste and garnish with chopped parsley. Rice, mashed potatoes, or pita bread are suitable as a side dish.

27.   Seitan Chips with Jerusalem Artichoke Puree

Preparation Time: 15 minutes

Cooking Time: 20 minutes

Servings: 4

Ingredients:

Seitan chips

250 g grilled seitan

Breadcrumbs

Yeast flakes

Corn oil

Ingredients for the Jerusalem Artichoke Puree:

250 g Jerusalem artichoke (3 - 4 tubers)

1 pinch of breadcrumbs

½ tsp Mediterranean spice mix

 1 pinch salt

2 tbsp shoyu (soy sauce)

1 tbsp olive oil

Directions:

1. Cut the seitan into thin slices, preferably with a slicer. In a container, mix the breadcrumbs and the yeast and bread the seitan slices.
2. Heat oil and fry slices on both sides until crispy. When golden, dry on absorbent kitchen paper.
3. Cut the Jerusalem artichokes into small cubes and fry in a pan with the oil, shoyu, a pinch of paprika, mixed spices, shoyu, and salt.
4. Simmer for about twenty minutes on low heat with a lid. Then whisk everything and add olive oil if necessary.

Enjoy your meal.

28.   Seitan Burger

Preparation Time: 15 minutes

Cooking Time: 20 minutes

Servings: 4

Ingredients:

200 g gluten

4 tbsp. yeast flakes

3 tbsp. soy sauce

2 tbsp. mustard

2 tbsp. tomato paste

1 tbsp. dried chili bell pepper

1 tbsp. lemon juice

1 tbsp. pear syrup

1 tsp. paprika powder

1 tsp. salt

1 tsp. pepper

2 shallots

5 tbsp. glutinous rice flour (from the Asian store)

2 red onions

4 tbsp. canola oil

4 sesame burger buns

2 handfuls arugula

4 tomato slices 4 tbsp vegan mayonnaise

Directions:

1. Mix gluten, yeast flakes, soy sauce, mustard, tomato paste, crushed chili pepper, lemon juice, pear syrup, spices, and 175 ml water to make a firm side batter and work well. Cook in steam for about 30 minutes. Allow to cool slightly.
2. Coarsely chop and grind in a blender to crumbly pieces to taste. Peel and chop shallots and knead into seitan mixture with glutinous rice flour and about 4 tbsp water. Form into 4 patties.

3. Cut onions into rings and fry with 2 tbsp of oil for about 10 minutes until crispy. At the same time, fry the patties for about 10 minutes until appetizing. At the same time, bake the rolls at 150° and cut them in half.

4. Spread ketchup on the underside of the rolls, top with arugula and tomato slice. Salt, pepper, and stack patties and crispy onions on top.

5. Top off with a tbsp of vegan mayonnaise to taste and place on top of the bun. Enjoy your meal!

Special Occasion Recipes

29. Seitan With Green Apple Relish

Preparation Time: 10 minutes

Cooking Time: 30 minutes

Servings: 4

Ingredients:

2 Granny Smith apples, coarsely chopped

½ cup finely chopped red onion

½ jalapeño chile, seeded and minced

1½ teaspoons grated fresh ginger

3 tablespoons fresh lime juice

2 teaspoons agave nectar

Salt and freshly ground black pepper

2 tbsp olive oil

1 pound seitan, homemade (see Basic Simmered Seitan) or store-bought, cut into 1⁄2-inch slices

Directions:

1. In a medium bowl, combine the apples, onion, chile, ginger, lime juice, agave nectar, and salt and pepper to taste. Set aside.
2. Heat the oil in a skillet over medium heat. Add the seitan and cook until browned on both sides, turning once, about 4 minutes per side. Season with salt and pepper to taste.
3. Add the apple juice and cook for a minute until it reduces. Serve immediately with the apple relish.

30. Seitan And Broccoli-Shiitake Stir-Fry

Preparation Time: 10 minutes

Cooking Time: 30 minutes

Servings: 4

Ingredients:

2 tablespoons canola or grapeseed oil

8 ounces seitan, homemade (see Basic Simmered Seitan) or store-bought, cut into 1/4-inch slices

3 garlic cloves, minced

2 teaspoons grated fresh ginger

3 green onions, minced

1 medium bunch broccoli, cut into 1-inch florets

3 tbsp soy sauce

2 tbsp dry sherry

1 teaspoon toasted sesame oil

1 tablespoon toasted sesame seeds

Directions:

1. In a large skillet, heat 1 tbsp of the oil over medium-high heat. Add the seitan and cook, stirring occasionally until lightly browned, about 3 minutes. Transfer the seitan to a bowl and set aside.
2. In the same skillet, heat the remaining 1 tablespoon of oil over medium-high heat. Add the mushrooms and cook, stirring frequently, until browned, about 3 minutes. Stir in the garlic, ginger, and green onions and cook 30 seconds longer. Add the mushroom mixture to the cooked seitan and set aside.
3. Add the broccoli and water to the same skillet. Cover and cook until the broccoli begins to turn bright green, about 3 minutes. Uncover and cook, stirring frequently, until the liquid evaporates and the broccoli is crisp-tender, about 3 minutes longer.
4. Return the seitan and mushroom mixture to the skillet. Add the soy sauce and sherry and stir-fry until the seitan and vegetables are hot, about 3 minutes. Sprinkle with the sesame oil and sesame seeds and serve immediately.

31.   Seitan Brochettes with Peaches And Herbs

Preparation Time: 10 minutes

Cooking Time: 30 minutes

Servings: 4

Ingredients:

⅓ cup balsamic vinegar

3 tablespoons dry red wine

3 tablespoons light brown sugar

¼ cup chopped fresh basil

¼ cup chopped fresh marjoram

2 tbsp minced garlic

3 tablespoons olive oil

1 pound seitan, homemade (see Basic Simmered Seitan) or store-bought, cut into 1-inch chunks

4 shallots, halved lengthwise and blanched

Salt and freshly ground black pepper

2 ripe peaches, pitted and cut into 1-inch chunks

Directions:

1. Combine the vinegar, wine, and sugar in a small saucepan and bring to a boil. Reduce heat to medium and simmer, stirring, until reduced by half, about 15 minutes. Remove from the heat.

2. In a large bowl, combine the basil, marjoram, garlic, and olive oil. Add the seitan, shallots, and peaches, and toss to coat. Season with salt and pepper to taste.

3. Preheat the grill. * Thread the seitan, shallots, and peaches onto the skewers and brush with the balsamic mixture.

4. Place the brochettes on the grill and cook until the seitan and peaches are grilled, about 3 minutes per side. Brush with the remaining balsamic mixture and serve immediately.

* Instead of grilling, you can put these brochettes under the broiler. Broil 4 to 5 inches from the heat until hot and lightly browned around the edges, about 10 minutes, turning once halfway through.

32. Grilled Seitan And Vegetable Kabobs

Preparation Time: 10 minutes

Cooking Time: 30 minutes

Servings: 4

Ingredients:

⅓ cup balsamic vinegar

2 tablespoons olive oil

1 tablespoon minced fresh oregano or 1 teaspoon dried

2 garlic cloves, minced

½ tsp salt

¼ teaspoon freshly ground black pepper

1 pound seitan, homemade (see Basic Simmered Seitan) or store-bought, cut into 1-inch cubes

8 ounces small white mushrooms, lightly rinsed and patted dry

2 small zucchini, cut into 1-inch chunks

1 medium yellow bell pepper, cut into 1-inch squares

12 ripe cherry tomatoes

Directions:

1. In a medium bowl, combine the vinegar, oil, oregano, thyme, garlic, salt, and black pepper.
2. Add the seitan, mushrooms, zucchini, bell pepper, and tomatoes, turning to coat. Marinate at room temperature for 30 minutes, turning occasionally. Drain the seitan and vegetables, reserving the marinade.
3. Preheat the grill. * Thread the seitan, mushrooms, and tomatoes onto skewers.
4. Place the skewers on the hot grill and cook, turning kabobs once halfway through grilling, about 10 minutes total. Drizzle with a small amount of the reserved marinade and serve immediately.

* Instead of grilling, you can put these skewers under the broiler. Broil 4 to 5 inches from the heat until hot and lightly browned around the edges, about 10 minutes, turning once halfway through broiling.

33.   TVP Teriyaki Burgers

Preparation Time: 10 minutes

Cooking Time: 30 minutes

Servings: 4

Ingredients:

1 cup textured vegetable protein

½ cup panko breadcrumbs

½ tsp salt

¼ tsp ground black pepper

¼ tsp garlic powder

¼ tsp onion powder

1 tbsp ketchup

¾ cup hot water

¼ cup teriyaki sauce

¼ cup all-purpose flour

2 tbsp olive oil

4 slices fresh pineapple

Directions:

1. In a large bowl, combine TVP, breadcrumbs, salt, pepper, garlic powder, onion powder, ketchup, and water. Let sit for 5 minutes.
2. Mix in flour and form in 4 equal-sized pieces.
3. Heat oil in a large skillet, cook patties until browned on both sides. Top burgers with pineapple slices.

34.   French Onion TVP Burgers

Preparation Time: 10 minutes

Cooking Time: 30 minutes

Servings: 4

Ingredients:

1 cup textured vegetable protein

½ cup panko breadcrumbs

4 tsp Italian seasoning

2 tbsp balsamic vinegar

¾ cup hot water

¼ cup all-purpose flour

4 tbsp olive oil, divided

1 small onion, sliced

4 slices vegan provolone cheese

Directions:

1. In a large bowl, combine TVP, breadcrumbs, seasoning, balsamic vinegar, and water. Let sit for 5 minutes.

2. Mix in flour and form into 4 equal-sized patties.
3. Heat 2 tbsp olive oil in a large skillet, add patties, and cook until browned on both sides.
4. In another skillet, add 2 tbsp olive oil and cook onions over medium-low heat until caramelized, about 15-20 minutes.
5. Top burgers with 1 slice of vegan cheese and onion mixture.

35. Black Bean Veggie Burgers

Preparation Time: 10 minutes

Cooking Time: 30 minutes

Servings: 4

Ingredients:

2 (15 ounces) cans black beans, drained

1 (15 ounces) can corn, drained

½ cup old fashioned oats

½ large onion, finely diced

2 tbsp ground flax seed

2 tbsp water

1 clove garlic, minced

½ tsp salt

¼ tsp ground black pepper

½ tsp chili powder

Directions:

1. In a large bowl, place all ingredients. Mash everything together with a potato masher until fully combined.
2. Using your hands, form the mixture into 8 equal-sized patties. Place onto a plate and set aside.
3. Either grill on an outdoor or indoor grill or cook in 2 tbsp olive oil over medium heat.

Sides Recipes

36. Seitan Spinach Mushroom Pilaf with Turmeric and Quinoa

Preparation Time: 10 minutes

Cooking Time: 40 minutes

Servings: 3

Ingredients:

<u>For the Pilaf:</u>

1 cup quinoa

3 cups vegetable broth

150 g frozen spinach leaves, thawed

100 g mushrooms

1 onion

100 g shitake mushrooms

2 tsp turmeric

150 g seasoned seitan in pieces

50 g almond slivers

450 ml vegetable broth

100 ml oat cream herbal salt sesame oil lemon juice

Directions:

1. Wash quinoa in a colander and cook in lightly simmering vegetable broth for 20 min, set aside.
2. Dry seitan and fry in oil. Roughly chop onions and sauté vigorously with seitan.
3. Halve shitake mushrooms, roughly slice mushrooms and sauté briefly with seitan.
4. Add frozen spinach with turmeric to the seitan and simmer with broth for about 10 minutes.
5. Season with herb salt and lemon juice and serve hot with quinoa.

37.   Seitan Wraps

Preparation Time: 10 minutes

Cooking Time: 40 minutes

Servings: 3

Ingredients:

Pilaw 3 wheat tortillas

1 zucchini

1 bell pepper (red)

2 garlic cloves

200g seitan some mustard

1 tomato some arugula or baby spinach (both delicious!) Optional: a few olives 1 onion some cane sugar

200g chickpeas (pre-cooked or from a jar)

Optional:

Some red chili

2 tbsp olive oil

2 tbsp cumin

2 tbsp black pepper

2 tbsp salt

Directions:

1. Cut the zucchini into thin slices of salt, mix and drain in a colander for at least half an hour. Dab off remaining moisture with kitchen paper.
2. Preheat oven to 250°C with grill.
3. Quarter and seed peppers, dice one clove of garlic, mix with olive oil, and place on baking paper in the oven. When the skin of peppers blisters or sufficient degree of browning, remove peppers from the oven and set them aside.
4. Meanwhile, cut seitan into strips and fry in oil until crispy, salt and pepper vigorously and add a little mustard at the end.
5. Sauté onion rings in the second pan until slightly translucent. Sprinkle in cane sugar and caramelize lightly.
6. Wash and dry arugula/spinach. Slice olives and tomatoes.
7. Puree chickpeas with second garlic clove some olive oil, chili, pepper, cumin, and a pinch of salt until creamy.
8. Spread chickpea cream on wraps, top with other ingredients, and roll up. Enjoy your meal!

Gravies, Sauces, And Glazes

38. Seitan Nuggets with Sweet Chili Sauce

Preparation Time: 10 minutes

Cooking Time: 40 minutes

Servings: 4

Ingredients:

500 g seitan

200 ml water

1 tbsp. coconut blossom sugar

300 g cane sugar

200 ml water

2 red chili peppers

1 yellow chili pepper

3 garlic cloves

1 small onion

1000 ml coconut oil

100 ml lime juice

1 cup flour

1 tbsp cornstarch

1 tbsp cornflakes

1 tbsp chili powder

1 pinch of black pepper

1 pinch sea salt

1 tbsp Paprika powder

Directions:

1. Cut the seitan into pieces for the nuggets (approx. 3x 5 cm), salt, and pepper generously.
2. Crumble the cornflakes in a bowl, set them aside.
3. Mix one part flour, one part starch, and gradually add water until you get a thick dough. Season this heavily with chili powder, paprika, pepper, sea salt, a little lime juice, and a tbsp of coconut blossom sugar.

For the Sauce:

4. Finely dice the garlic cloves and the onion. Sauté thin slices of the chilies, along with the garlic and onion in a saucepan in some coconut oil until lightly brown.
5. Now add coconut blossom sugar and let it caramelize briefly. Deglaze with water and lime juice.
6. Let the liquid evaporate until a creamy mass is formed. Season to taste with sea salt and pepper. Cool in a serving bowl.
7. Heat the coconut oil to about 180 °C for frying. Pull the seitan pieces through the batter, then roll them in the cornflakes and deep-fry until they have reached the desired degree of browning. Serve hot with chili sauce.

39.   Seitan with Tomatillo Sauce

Preparation Time: 15 minutes

Cooking Time: 30-120 minutes

Servings: 10

Ingredients:

4 cups cubed chicken-flavored seitan

1 ⅔ pounds tomatillos, husked and chopped

1 can green chilis

3 cloves garlic, minced

¼ cup apple cider vinegar

1 tsp salt

2 tsp chili powder

½ tsp cumin

¼ tsp coriander

1 tsp olive oil

¼ cup water

Juice of 1 lime

Directions:

1. Add everything except the seitan to a food processor and blend to make the sauce.
2. Add the sauce and the seitan to the instant pot. Seal the lid and cook on high for 4 minutes, then let the pressure release naturally.
3. Serve in warm tortillas or over a bed of rice.

Conclusion

Congratulations on making it this far. Vital wheat gluten is a flour made from only the gluten of the wheat kernel, with starch, hull, germ, and bran washed away, then dried and ground into flour. This is the thickening part of wheat and is what holds bread together.

Gluten dough is vital wheat gluten mixed with liquid to form a dough which is very elastic and kind of strange to work with until you get used to it. It has a mind of its own and is not as easy to knead or form as regular bread dough. Don't worry about it – it will fight back and have crevices and seams and won't look exactly smooth and pretty, but it evens itself out over time.

CPSIA information can be obtained
at www.ICGtesting.com
Printed in the USA
LVHW050544260621
691140LV00012B/1923